Waking in Winter

GW01072018

Waking in Winter

Anna Wigley

Gomer

Published in 2009 by Gomer Press, Llandysul,
Ceredigion SA44 4JL

ISBN 978 1 84323 970 3
A CIP record for this title is available from the British Library.

This book is published with the financial support of the
Welsh Books Council.

Printed and bound in Wales at
Gomer Press, Llandysul, Ceredigion

for Huw

ACKNOWLEDGEMENTS

Some of these poems first appeared in *Planet* magazine and in *Poetry Wales*. The author would like to thank the editors for permission to publish them in this collection.

CONTENTS

Learning to Swim

For Si

The smell of ferns that summer:
a green musk, with the tang of streams
cobbled with birds'-egg pebbles,
and the jungle heat of a July noon.

The ferns were cool to the touch
and sprang back from our tugging hands
as we waded thigh-deep
through their soft green breakers.

Wooded with their stems, the hill
rustled softly in the wind.
Not an inch was uncovered,
not a patch of ground

remained unroofed by tiles
of tapering fronds. Drops of sun
dripped through the tiny cracks
in the long green feathers

but the rest was caught and cabled
in the vast factory of ferns.
You threw me into a plashy pool
of leaves, and I screamed,

feeling the sky tilt sharply
and the hill jerk up
to break my bones;
then suddenly found I could swim.

Daisies

On wetted, brilliant verges,
scatterings of wind-harried daisies,
their lipsticked petals pursed,
their thin stems frailer than grass.

It's as if they have found me
after thirty years; the same daisies
on the same small banks of turf:
child-sized flowers with plain hearts.

However much we trampled them,
our bare toes snagging the stalks,
or snicked them by the necklace-load,
slicing an eyelet for threads,
they always returned in abundance,
a foaming galaxy of stars.

Earlier than the roses, they
were the first hushed voices of summer –
fresh as the thin May showers
that slicked their early crops –

then later, in June, July,
old familiar friends, setting off
the operatic roses and lilies
with a pure astringent note,
their chaste, plainsong hosannas.

Poplar

There's a mountain stream in that tree,
a hurry of flashing water
lacing over tidefalls of small stones,
twisting the light to a silverwork
of brilliant shards: weightless scraps
of beaten metal
tethered by one frail thread
to the mountain-hump of the poplar trunk.
Even in the faintest bird-breath breeze
the bright stream trembles,
and sighs with the soft exhalation
of thin water
wooing a million shell-frail stones.

Return to Llangennith

Here the light chisels everything clean:
the wavy treads of tyres, knotted ropes of a garden swing,
the delicate feet of sheep, a tussock's nap,
and all the brushed-out, wispy ends of trees
that spread their chandeliers for the crows.

What a day! A day like those
when fern-spires crumpled in our fists
and the gorse never tired or grew dim.

Ram

One black leather hoof
is all that's left whole
near the rag of wool.

In the nest of ribs
flies sup and pool;
the guts are drying
their snaky spill;

the eyes have dropped
their soft ripe fruits
to the blackened soil.

For ten days now
he's been the spoil
of beetle and crow;

pale summer sun
has lightly cooked
his banquet of coils,
the steaks of muscle.

And there's something peaceful
in his lack of will,
his gift of himself
to the hungriest worm
– like a fallen apple.

Kittening

For two days she had been gone;
restless at her blood's command
to nose out some sheltered cave, and lay
the nippled hill of her belly down.

When we found her there were already two:
licked skulls and sealed eyes
clamped to her side. She gazed
cloudily inwards, surrendered
to her own thick bliss. And presently

a third, then a fourth gleaming sac
slipped from her in dumb shock.
She turned to lick them as if
tidying some morsel she'd dropped.

Squatting at the threshold
of her cupboard, we felt like visitors
to some Biblical scene
domesticated in a corner:
Lazarus rising from his bed of twenty years
while his wife cooked breakfast next door.

Oak

New leaves
clump on the oak:

the old twister,
frilled and tender,

fishes in the lake
of light, its nets

fronding from painters
of stalks

to catch and sift
bright from dark.

We stand
in the shadow

of its scales,
reach hands

to the barrel chest
of the trunk

and look up
as pilgrims have

always, but
clamp our feet

firm, to the root-
rich bible of earth.

Buzzard

His mewing is a cry to the clouds
where he traces shallow spirals
without hurry or strain,
testing the tips of his reach
as an octopus at rest blossoms
to a tender, many-spoked wheel.

He seems not to watch but to sail
complete in the ocean of his silence,
drawing the exquisite circles
like a painter using himself
as the brush, stroking the sky's canvas
with dark-barred bristles.

How he feels the air!
The currents, invisible and firm,
bear his broad chariot
with muscular breath,
turning up the ligaments
and tendons of woods and fields.

Even when he falls, he drops
like water swirling round a hole,
never breaking for a moment the slow
rhythm of his curving glide;
seeming less to dive than to faint
earthwards, a soundless kite
no longer lifted by the wind.

St Govan's Chapel

Over a twist of black silk steps
slicing the downward spill of rock,
the grass stops short.
And there at the foot
wedged between cliff-flanks,
is a stone roof burying its snout
in slabbed boulders. It seems
welded in fast and eyeless.

But creep right down to the low brow
of the tiled edge,
and you are Alice,
stooping at the entrance
to a troglodyte's lair:
a plain cool square hollowed from the cliff's gut.

A single small window
frames a blaze of sea; a ledge
supports wildflowers in a cup.

From limestone passageways
you'll peep like an oyster
from its shell, onto a savage bay.
No beach here, no soft sand; nothing
but a few hanks of grass and samphire
stitched into stone cracks.

Below you the shore
crumbles to a quick death;
the water, green and sheer,
cuffs and smacks at the cliff-roots.
There is nowhere to go:
the chapel with its thick short bones
and unblinking eye, is where it ends.

Peat Bog Bodies, Dublin Museum

If they could look at us, what would they think?
Perhaps that, modern Egyptians, we revered
bodies preserved like lemons; lifting with tender touch
the leathery remains, to these transparent graves.
So much extravagant care taken –
the peat washed off with kisses, the remarkable hands
laid out just so, under lights only bright enough
to pick out the acid-ochred pores of skin.
Each body lies in its own whorled temple, flesh within a shell.
We scavenge on forbidden fruit:
the severed edge of a torso, a last meal of lentils.
Three deaths, this last one suffered,
with torque and noose and blade,
an unholy trinity of intrusions.
Looking at us, fastidious grave-robbers,
the peat bog men – incomplete, dishonoured –
might find us also lacking in something:
a leaving of the dead to their secrets,
this loose untidy dress of flesh, with all its buttons broken.

Avebury

You read the landscape like a body:
ridges, contours, knolls, that are to me
uninteresting bulges, pretty or strange at most,
are to you the bones of ages lost.

We see the plains for miles around;
the roads that seam the flat expanse of ground
converge on us. The accidental lines
assume a shape: there is the spine

that holds the other pathways up.
I listen; and as I do, your voice is like a rope
thrown down the centuries. It binds
me a little more closely to the land

that had seemed plain and featureless before.
I look at you and squeeze your hand. Another door
yawns wide for me to walk through; you
are as broad and as long as the centuries too.

Bernard Llewellyn

We found you among the mud and the hard cries of lambs.
Hair wetted to your brow with slog,
you greeted us, beaming
as if we were long-lost uncles,
your hand too rank to shake.
Behind you the ewes and their lambs
snuggled tight to each other's haunches,
and when you plucked one out,
I saw how she suddenly forgot her fear
and was meek when you held her
with thirty years of knowing just the place
to wrench her fleece between your fingers
and keep her tranced, while you ploughed the wool
with the magic chisel of the shears.
The smell of the work poured off you
stronger than cheap aftershave; the tang of dung,
the rich stew of straw and clay and shit
spattered you as it sprayed everything.
Beside you, the cotton bag held a year's worth
of wool, the sheep's spent husks.
They scampered off one by one,
all pinched and closely barbered
as poor boys scalped for a couple of quid,
pink skin showing through the stubble.

Miserable Weather

The weatherman forecasts miserable weather.
By this he means grey, my favourite colour
for skies: the radiant pewter and soft,
fraying violet of Welsh rain-clouds,
their quilted palaces and hills heaped
low over the fields, dragging blue shadows.
And by miserable he means rain:
the liquid god, answer to prayers
in the fevered dreams of farmers;
turner of keys in the soil, flicker of switches,
master of resurrections, waking the pip,
the tiny flakes, the weightless grains
and almost invisible dots from their virgin sleep.
Miserable weather puts fat on the sheep.
Miserable weather swells corn, oats and barley.
The clouds sag with riches,
the fields brim with ingots, and every ditch
is an open purse, spilling silver.
Let miserable weather run in the streets
like a mad girl, tossing her long hair.
Let it pass its hand over the hills
and heal their arid sleep.
Miserable weather is our birthright: we grew up
to the sound of pattering on roofs,
the gurgled song of gutters.
We learned to put on kitchen lights
on summer mornings, and wear umbrellas
everywhere, like second skins.
Our fridges are crammed with butter,
cheese and cream. From our taps
the miserable weather gushes in hot and cold streams;
in the rose-bed scatters masterpieces.

Recording

To the memory of my father

Suddenly he is here, in the room.
I crouch close to the winding spool,
to catch the drops of him.

He's speaking under a sea-storm;
I strain to sight the contours
of sentences through the mists.

Winnowing his sounds
like lost treasure, I make out
clean Welsh edges to his words

and that habit of fairness I'd forgotten:
the way he'd treat the smallest subject
with a principled respect

then, justice done,
dismiss it with a flick of wit,
blink brightly; and move on.

Catching a Peach

Peaches heaped in the shops at last:
each a sunset of faded gold
sinking in dusty purple clouds.

I buy five, testing the flesh,
honeying my nose.
I try to imagine a peach tree grove,
where branches sag with sweetness
and the ground is suedey with fruit.

But one peach after all
is enough –
one dark and heavy with juice,
with a little too much rouge,

staining the fingers red-wet.
That fruit must be caught like a trout.
Pears have one perfect day;
peaches one perfect minute.

Good Company

Lias, you said; it's lias.
And the cliffs where we had walked
among tumbled alabaster
and slabs of fudgy slate
had faces and names.

Into a ball you rolled the aeons,
their plasticine folds.

Here's Cambrian and Jurassic –
rub between finger and thumb
this pinch of desert
where leather wings flapped.
And here's the mollusc's fan
sculpted in its tomb of rock.

Your nails were lined with dirt,
moulded clean as fossils.

Pointing to a sparkle of dust
precious in a pebble,
you spoke rare words
in ancient dialects –

the glaciers swam behind your eyes,
the amber forests.
Skins of limestone and granite
showed you their finest pores.

Jan, you have eyes
the colour of waves on a winter beach,
hands that could tame dinosaurs.

Stephen

He had a slightly drunken walk,
for death, amusing himself,
had cuffed him once or twice;

and now he went with a hiccuping step,
mind fierce on the loose faggot
of limbs; the stair's cliff-face.

His pallor showed he was on short loan.
Pale lips, pale eyes spoke
of an overdue appointment somewhere else.

And his body was the ramshackle house
he'd got lumbered with:
rotting timbers, rising damp.

It was the place where his voice lived,
only half surviving its passage
to the outside world. Yet out

tumbled the words, thickened and quick,
thrown off like showers of sparks
from some forge diabolically hot.

Now all snuffed out. The bright blaze
smothered, the furnace cold.
But his kindnesses left

well-wrought and intact.
And the body at last given back,
like a suit that had never quite fitted.

Lotuses

*Golden Lotuses was the name given to the bound feet
of Chinese women*

Bind them tight, Mother, bind them tight!
Don't let that toe escape! Oh, but at night
I weaken, Mother; I loosen the bandages
and gaze at my golden lotuses.

You have tended them well, the soil is good.
The little hoofs are humping coyly
over the neatly folded arches.
Mother, I have no toes! Those fleshy claws
are tucked away like bad thoughts.

Strange, when I ran in the fields
like a boy, grass tickling my soles.
I was a baby then. My skirts flew,
my legs knew no better than to run.

I had not learned what perfumes
the flesh can brew, how sweet the rot
can rise in the nostrils of a bridegroom.
My feet grew straight; I flexed them
when it pleased me, like a smile.

That was before the grandmothers came
with their kind eyes and mile of ribbon.
In peacock silk the delicate snouts
of their trotters peeped out.

I saw my husband's face reflected
in their slippers' embroidered roses;
I saw him lift me
like a bouquet of cut flowers.

So don't cry, Mother, don't cry.
A woman with feet is no woman.
I'm afraid my rags grow slack.
Bind them tight as I can bear, now,
and in time the lotuses will blossom.

Scholar

School to him was a dead river
where his silver soul floated

with its bright eye clouded
in the stagnant water.

But at home, in the shed,
were his birds: the blazing books

where at night he bent his head
to read talon and feather

and gaze on the letters
of their gold and emerald looks.

What could a classroom teach him
of the lure and jess,

the glove both flexible and thick,
the hood as intricately pieced

as a lacquered terrapin?
These were his ruler and compass,

his chalk and pen.
The hours vanished

into silence,
as he tended and crouched

over his charges, and coaxed
wilderness into his hand.

A kestrel clamped his fingers
and stared like the Spanish sun;

its breast of speckled feathers
tested him: what could explain

such a glut of perfection?
Daily he feasted on mysteries

like these, and never thought
himself a scholar, even then.

But he studied weather:
the black frost over his shoulders,

and the birds' cold plumage
in the dark as he carried them;

the glory of the fields and woods
where high trees waited

to be rustled and gripped
by the sharp feet of his creatures.

He sensed the laws of physics
in a spread wing: the harmony

of filament with current,
or the way his mind would break,

stalled, against the weight
of its own forward movement

when he entered the school gates.
He kept himself for dusk

and the hut where marvels perched,
blinking on their branches,

waiting for his voice's
first cooing touch.

Byways

On summer Sunday afternoons
they call to me, the ragged lanes
and plain, high garden walls
where frugal weeds feasting on stones
spiral and nod and dip their cones.

If I follow them long enough
there's a barred iron gate
that judders rust when I mount it
to reach a rubbled, ragwort track.

Here no one walks; the soft batting
of small birds startled from their hides,
and my hot feet on the hotter stones
is all I hear. That, and somewhere near,

invisible, a rope of water
twining its braid between the steep flanks
of swelling grass, where the little water flowers grow
unregarded, perfect as love-children.

Skylight

All night the open skylight made a window in your dreams
for the bushy silences of wood and sky
to waft through, drifting their soil-smell and sheep-cries.

Next to me you stirred like a baby
snuffling at his pillow.
You suckled at sleep, you were starved for it
and your face was slack with longing.
Over the bed the air blew its muslin,
kissing your stubbled cheek; and the trees called
softly with voices of resin and a shudder of warm leaves.

Small birds partook of your dreams, and all the velvet creatures –
saucer-eyed mice and stealthy night-warriors –
borne in on that balmy current to mingle their colours
on the canvas of your sleep, with fragments of old lovers,
spots and flecks of the day just gone, and purple-tinted fears.

The Missing Cats of Roath

Tacked to the makeshift noticeboards
of lamp-posts and trees,
their blurred, faded faces peer out
at passing strangers, like whiskered babies
stolen from their prams;
or once-prosperous refugees,
now wandering the world of back lanes
barefoot, without a passport or a name.
They are the missing cats of Roath,
the lost links in a chain of cats
that curls from Angus to Arabella Street
and back; cats guarding their dignity
in smutty gutters, on crumbling walls,
or framed in windows where once a day
a lozenge of sunlight falls.
Please check your garages and sheds
the posters plead, for Tigger, Molly and Fred,
for Nipper, Fluffy and Nutmeg,
who may be kipping there under an old rake
in a nest of cobwebs, smeared with oil,
already getting that mangy look, those haunted eyes,
reverting to feral versions of themselves,
slaking their thirst on rain puddles,
and after years of indolence and Kit-e-Kat,
pricking their ears at tiny scurryings
and learning, at last, to hunt.
But somehow they never turn up,
the missing cats of Roath.
They are too numerous; it can't be chance
that so many end like this: famous for a week,
their pictures hung up as talismans, idols,
messages to the gods.
Somewhere they congregate, and smile at us.
Somewhere, they curl into perfect circles, and wait.

A Peeled Satsuma for Marilou

Marilou, I offer you this segment
picked clean of pith, as small
and plump and richly coloured
as yourself; as shiny, I hope,
as the fruit you offered me once –

that day when I noticed your sun
had been eclipsed, and some dark doubt,
some bitter tiredness, etched shadows
under your eyes (polished coffee beans
set slantwise in the satin of your face):

Have one of these, you said,
holding out the small gleaming fruit,
It's all right, they're sweet –
seeing me hesitate perhaps, accustomed
to the wary ways of foreigners,
their failure to take the proffered food,
to open and eat the satsuma of peace;

and so, because I said no,
and because you have bloomed like a tiger lily
among the wood spurge and chickweed
of this forest far from home,
I offer you this fragment, Marilou,
to swallow whole, or to burst
with your perfect teeth, and chew.

For a Young Gull Injured in Roath Park

Cruel conjunction of metal and feather,
of bright new eye and hot exhaust,
of piston and slender foot.

Herring-gull, with your mottled plumage
the colour of rain-smudged skies in November,
and unfledged steps
that had known only the cold cushion
of water, and the gentle admonishments
of twigs and roots –

why did you blunder at precisely that moment
into the road's death-mill,
when one learner driver
as wobbly and unpractised as yourself
hesitated towards you, then

picked up speed and went right over.
Tumbled in the undercarriage
you recovered your balance, almost,
before another car, then another

drove over you as if you were nothing
but a bundle of blown chip-papers.
And still you were not dead, quite.
Herring-gull, with your sleek head
and wings just turning to cadmium,

wings that should have lifted you clear
of voracious tin-box gods
with their dead-eyed sovereignty;
you were a child's finger
caught in a factory wheel,

mere roadkill, our name
for all soft, dazzled creatures
whose crime is to wander unknowing
into the path of those who cannot fly, and so must,
at all costs, keep moving, and without delay.

The Yellow Years

Those were the yellow years.
After you left I began
to stain at the corners.

A few curious souls
took me down from the shelf.
They turned me with clumsy fingers.

I smelt of dust.
I watched two men pass by:
my rice-paper leaves shivered,

but they left me shut.
My story was still locked up
waiting to be read.

I'd run it past you once:
you thought the plot bad.
You put me back.

I waited for other hands,
other eyes. But those
were the yellow years. None stopped.

Outpatient

He is there in all weathers:
plimsoll laces dragging, jacket sagging,
fifth fag of the morning glowing
from between uncertain fingers.

Like me, he's waiting for the train,
alert for the nearing growl and rumble,
shuffling to the platform edge and back,
alone in his Rothmans cumulus
and whatever signs reach his universe.

Yet, of the two of us, he is the one
who reaches out, barking a rough greeting
then mumbling at his cigarette and muttering
half to me, half to himself,
hardly caring if the words hit their mark.

If he wonders at the slowness
of my understanding, he doesn't show it,
but repeats his jumbled message over and over,
like birds, or a dog, or a lover.

To Josh

May I never take too much care of you.
May you always have lumps of tar
clotting your coat,
and coaldust sooting your paws,
the scent of rats' fur on your breath.

Nonetheless I wish you
to go daintily among dangers,
to stay aloof from loud noises
and the road's roulette.
Avoid your kind:
they know where to sink a tooth.
Be wary of boys, their ways
cannot be trusted.

But may I never keep you so safe
that your claws grow blunt
and your eyes lose their threat.
Let there be many long nights

when you do not return
however long I call into the darkness;
when, for the space of a moon,
you no longer answer to your name.

Henna

Temple prostitutes used you –
the men smelling hair like earth,
murmuring prayers into the red silk.
Surely Eve's apple had your hue.

Henna, your heritage is venerable
and ancient as the musk that rises
as I tip out the bag,
sniffing at the powdered dung.

How many women in palaces and tenements,
in bedsits and locked bathrooms,
have performed your ministries:
mixing like artists the glossy paste,
staining ears and fingers orange,
plastering their heads with the thick green icing,

feeling the crumbs and soft clumps fall
to blot the porcelain's chaste bowl.
Harmless vanity; yet once your name
meant sluts and tarts, and vices
dark and deep as your auburn stain.

Now hippies and artists have reclaimed you,
your messy ritual rescued from hairdressers' salons
and the adman's rank ammonias.
We buy you by the ounce from health stores,
stash the sludge-dark ash in wooden drawers
like precious spices.
You are the wise woman's friend,
the pagan's favourite.

And we go on using you for far too long,
our straggling locks dyed chilli and cinnamon
long after our skin and eyes have sunk and faded.

Potter

She spins from clods
the colour of rivers on rainy days
her spheres,

coaxing them up
from an obdurate flatness,
the slip gloving her fingers
as the bowl is urged to blossom,
and from nothing the grooves appear.

Under the wideness of her eyes
and the crouching of her body –
half working, half waiting –
the clay aspires
to a fine unbroken curve.

The spoon of her red raw hand
supports it, encourages a flare
like the full hip of a tulip.

Then at once she sees it is done,
a pot is formed. The wheel halts
and there stands the new, dizzy clay
in its muddy caul.

Later when she takes it from the fire
she will give it a skin of stone-colour
and set it in a window
where the light will complete it –
scything its edges,
throwing an anchor of shadow.

The Fox Fur

The only time I got to see a fox
was when my grandmother,
famed for her elegance, wore
not one, but two round her neck.

I'd seen pictures of tribal warriors
with remote, silent eyes
shrugging the trophy-skins of deer
and buffalo over their shoulders;

my grandmother's hauteur
was not so different from theirs.
The long narrow pelts
of glistening cinnamon hairs

swung heavily over her breasts
of fine, tailored wool.
There was the fitful ghost
of an animal reek

under the sweet clogging
of talcum and perfume.
If she had not also carried
an invisible skin of ice

I might have stretched a hand
to stroke the fox's silk.
But the feet that dangled like pegs
and the terrible tiny face

still staring inward with shock,
were those of my grandmother's
stiff body, snowed eyes
under a brilliant coat.

Hosanna

Dogs in the park on a day in late October
are crazed with their own discoveries:
the way a drift of leaves can be bull-charged
like a new element, one that scatters itself
noisily; the nip that whites their breath
and squeezes the trigger of their legs;
the air's brilliance; other dogs –
barely keeping up with their own speed,
intoxicated by the light and a ball's
sudden promise of satisfaction,
stopping short in mid-dash,
standing foursquare with a lifetime's attention
to some thin ethereal whistle, or teasing
down-funnelling leaf. A Jack Russell
smooth and nubby as a bone, streaks towards nothing,
finds it, sniffs a stone,
then with delicate sips takes the bouquet
of a husky's buttocks. Nothing is too small
or great for their extravagant amusement
and delight, squandered in gestures large
with energy's caricaturing talent.
With the pert intelligence of their cocked tails,
quivering hind legs, they sing their praises.

Dreaming for Porsche

He's following them at night now
like a lover tracking their moves
as they ride loose spirals
to the tops of hills, at sunset
or under thunder-shadowed skies.

They pull him in their wake
as if he's on skis
and the movement is noiseless and smooth.
There are no trees, no wind,
just bare land to be doodled on
and a song from the Sixties.

For fifteen years he's been dreaming
for the company, spinning wheels
across slim bones of bridges,
through always deserted streets
lined with tall Spanish houses,
and the women within them waiting
for the mating call of the engine.

In his dream nobody stalls.
The capsule speeds rocket-like
through desert and forest
unscarred by roads.
In his nightmares a man
astride a hurtling box of wires
perches like a fly on dung.

Baking Day in Candleford

Husband, I have baked you a pie.
A pie such as Scheherezade
might have made
to divert the king's knife.

The butter was of the finest,
churned from the cow whose flank
you liked to sting with flicks
when the milk baulked.

I milled the flour myself,
plucked fat ears from the field
where the stalks grew tall
as riding crops.

No trouble was too much.
I made the mixture rich
with yolks; put my fingers in ice
before I eased in the fat.

From the offcuts I scalloped
a tricorn tulip,
its golden stem curling
like a narrow bull-whip.

You look surprised.
Was it your beating last night
that has made me pliant?
Today's the day a year ago

you first took out your belt.
Since then I've become quite cosy
with the kiss of the lash.
Up my spine there's a welt

like a cobra; and a dint
in my nape where the buckle went.
It has taught me a lesson,
it has made me wise.

So, husband, cut open my pie.
Inside you will find curled tight
an old poisonous snake that once
held your falling trousers up.

Shop Girls

At this chilled hour
of the small cold moon
and the sun a lagoon
of dirty orange iron

the streets are ours.
Cocooned in our wools,
hair bright as new coins,

we break the pavement's membrane
of cold white sleep
as we hurry to our stations.

The frost cannot disturb
our gilded cheeks and noses,
our shimmering calves,
our nails like tiny shells
rinsed and glossed by the tides.

Soon the wafting doors
will bear us in: a heaven
clocking in its angels.
The brilliantined floors
wait for the click and clatter
of our castanet shoes;

and tills line up in twos
like horses we will stroke
and slap for seven hours,
coaxing them over fence after fence.

November 5th

The streets are wet with lamplight
and my shoes are sticky with leaves
fallen rusty from the beeches.

Everything shines with darkness:
black railings, roof slates,
passing lanterns of faces

and through the yellow spotlights,
tiny rain, needle-thin,
stitching its splinters.

The night is pocked with dynamite
yapping above house-tops
and fizzing into momentary comets;

tomorrow will be damp carbon,
spent cartridges on lawns
and a squalor of leaves.

But now it is good to be walking
towards the golden windows,
through the excitable evening

with frost in my hair
and rain on my fingers,
all past Novembers stored in me
and in this night, like rings.

Offerings

You bring me trinkets, sweetmeats, treats –
the jewelled outriders of your love.
You, who are so unadorned in your dealings
and your dress; who will not wear pink
for fear it may mar your perfect plainness;
you bring me the small, heavy packets
loyally, routinely, without fanfare or flourish,
like a pagan propitiating a homely goddess,
one who is relied on to keep water running,
fridges humming, a new cake of soap in its dish.
Unwrapped, the offerings coil in my palm,
cool lustrous asps with agate eyes,
that later will embroider an earlobe, an arm.

Mementos

The buckles and hasps glint from their frills of rust.
A jug still lifts its swelling breast;
a sword frays to dirty lace.
Helmets raise their ragged shells;
brooches are crammed with garnet roe.
Odours of ancient dust
rise from the untouchable capsules.
We go on whispering feet
from blackened crocks to rudimentary ladles,
meagre congregations of tunic pins,
through tarnished constellations of small coins,
so thin they'd float like leaves on water.
Home again, I look at the picture of you as you were,
with hair that shone with the colours
of polished rosewood and mahogany.
Your eyes, if it were possible, were more blue.

Waking in Winter

From my bed I can feel how empty are the streets.
Nor does the house stir, but turns in darkness
while the windows sort their blurs from shadow
and frame the melting ice-slice of the moon.
The Christmases of childhood press in,
comforts of wool and tea, the brave corollas of cooker flame,
the painted garden visible from the kitchen
all spellbound; and a white smoke rising from the stones.
The night, then, kept its pact with the season,
was delivered while we slept to austerities of crystal,
the brushwork of a master.
Later, when I step out, I am a guest newly arrived
in a strange place, where the sun is made of pewter
and every brick and flag is sewn with sequins.

Solstice

We bring a branch of holly from the hill.
It smells of cold earth and a hard rind of moon.
It gleams with the health of a hardy, spartan thing.
There is sap ambering your hand where you held it
aloft, a ragged cross splintering the sun.
Now the room smells of spikes,
of the astringent, rustling woods.
Sap zings lightly in the air.
The holly leaves fill the space with their jagged foreign tongue.
We prop the branch in a corner, a shrine
to chilly-hearted evergreens, far stars
sharp as hatpin stones.

Used

Only when they've been thrown out
onto wet January pavements

is it possible to see how lovely
are the Christmas trees:

their silvery undersides showing like bloomers,
the swell of branches from the root, and the way

they bell out, thick and soft,
their needles still dense and polished,
their trunks as thick as pythons . . .

inches from the road they lie for days,
ignored, without crutches
or any kind of dignified farewell

allowed them; they simply get in the way.
They have been

intensely desired, and three weeks later
they lie upturned in the gutter

with their fannies showing
and a cold wind blowing.

The Fly

A fly drills and sizzles at the window,
crawls into silence, then drills again.
Like my thoughts of you
he seems to die for whole minutes,
then, just when you think he's gone,
has another fuss and crackle at the glass,
stupid as ever.

Mythical Houses

There are certain trees in certain streets
on winter afternoons; particular windows,
lit from within, in particular houses;
turnings that give suddenly
onto views of gelid laurels and icy terraces;

or whole parks laid out like open exhibitions
of their own most recent work,
unframed canvases of a Puritan austerity;

paving stones rising with their cracked spines
out of a milling mist underfoot;
and solitary crows, epic with the season
in their sharp coats and jousting helmets;

but most of all those certain streets
long-remembered; streets where the houses
are so solid, sure and self-possessed
they seem to have no inhabitants –

or none that come out; for who would want
to leave such houses? They stand
behind scrolled-iron gates and tall box-hedges,
like well-groomed, comfortable bachelors,

yet mysterious in the gently milling fog,
mortared with secrets. What do they know,
the houses? I pass them slowly,
watching. I know, without checking,

that inside each is a tangled wood,
a prince and a princess,
three dwarves, a witch with a nose-wart,
and two wolves asleep on the hearth,
next to the TV and the carpet slippers.

Visitors

They sat at my kitchen table,
the two polite Iranian academics,
and spoke politely of hangings and beheadings,
of chopped-off hands, and how
each stone for the stoning of adulteresses
was measured to state-decreed standards.
I'd been slicing onions when they arrived,
stuffing peppers for an evening meal,
with a glass of cold wine at my elbow, and talk
from a game-show twittering from the radio.
I looked at my unmarked wrists
and reflected on my many fornications.
I stroked my neck, and thought of demonstrations
when I'd marched under London skies, risking nothing
but a little boredom at the feeble, half-hearted
nature of our chanting. My tomcat –
felon, philanderer, and flouter of rules –
weaved freely between the legs of the two men,
promiscuously charming. When they left,
carrying their book of horrors, their careful
petitions, their cheques, I turned back
to my bright, messy kitchen,
where papers held news of pay-deals and taxes,
and knives were for cooking with.

Tea

Three bags in one cup, is how my father took it.
The war and a Welsh mother had got him used
to the oxtail soup of his brew.

Now, tea is like a mugful of history.
I sip at coalmining towns, cold front rooms,
at Hitler, the Home Guard, and desert.

Life without tea is a church without a graveyard,
a house without the deeds.
The Russians have their samovars,

we, our buxom lidded bowls.
Each is a portable piece of home,
a little tardis which, when we open it,

rushes at us with the smell of years
stretching forward and back, the steam
rising from all our lost childhoods.

When ill, I wanted nothing else.
Eloquent, it was passed to me
by every kind stranger,

sturdy as lint and Dettol.
Medicine for the soul, wholesome comforter,
tea, may you never forsake me

when I call on your poultice,
your promise of safety,
your sweet, strong, sheltering heat.

Appointment

You were taken in April

trees trembled
in a dream of tender leafings
parchments cracking open
on the thin cheroots of silk

there was a tricking wind
a wind that snatched then slept
and woke to swirl its skirts around your head
your small uncovered head

a bus stopped by the house
perhaps, and maybe you looked up
to the momentary faces
maybe you looked up

to the brash and brawny skies
trailing their winter rags
and felt the air lift your hair, felt April
blow cold on your small soft neck

at your elbow the new buds
swelling, sealed and hard
offered no interest in your passing,

no help; pranged by the wind
they slept with their secrets

the day held so many secrets
not even you were told
what the minutes prepared in their bud.

The Baton

How smoothly you handed on the baton.
As if you'd known the time and place
and kept it secret from us; then
when the moment came, yielded it up
saying *Take it, quick, I cannot hold it,*
and let it swiftly slip your grasp.
We were left looking down at your empty hands,
the worn, surrendered fingers,
and a weight that had suddenly shifted.

Transformation

Now you are kin to flowers and grass:
the crumpled head of a daisy snicked from its root,
the hank of cut lawn drying to straw.
We all saw it so plainly there
on the hospital bed: your bruised shell,
your poor nose pinched and yellow.
How immeasurably you were beyond us,
translated to a husk, a dropped leaf.
No time, no notice given.
Not even you were informed.

No Longer at This Address

The letters arrive like the last leaves falling
from the tree that bore your name.
I sweep them up from the mat,
these envelopes that have not heard,
that remind you when your licence expires,
or offer you better deals on this or that.
There is nothing now to renew,
the trunk and the roots are cut.
Your money worries are finished,
the last bills paid, the seasons halted.
Your replies were always prompt,
you filed your papers in drawers,
a neatly sectioned cabinet.
How ordered you were in your affairs,
and how quickly, quietly, you left.

Last Words

These drawers, where your things lie folded
as you left them, waiting to be worn,
crank open like doors between two worlds:

this one, filled with traces, imprints, signs,
like empty birds' nests, perfect and deserted;
and that other where you walked and breathed,

and washed and ironed these small handkerchiefs.
Here they lie, neat and smooth and ordered,
eloquent as last words, and yet

you never intended them as such.
One day you pressed them, flattened their corners,
and stored them prettily in this box –

a small, accidental epitaph.
In the bathroom are your lipsticks,
their wax seals gathering dust.

Snow

February, and snow dithers down fast,
wetting the bent heads of the snowdrops.
It is falling, too, a mile from here,
in your bedroom, on the unmarked grave,
on the heavy sheets and pillows of earth.
Many quiet months have passed,
months when memory has stood and looked
and made you again as you were,
weaving its hesitant epitaphs.
This house contains you still,
and in the garden the flowers you planted bloom
everywhere, in mute, belated tributes.
Your stone, too, will be dumb
but lovely as we can make it, from slate
as smooth as vellum,
the colour of dirty snow –
a plain grey page with your name on.

Flags

Bright-sworded, Alpine weather,
and your cyclamens, the small ones,
with cold-stung, pink-stained cheeks,
have slowly, slowly blossomed.
You loved them especially,
their flaring Indian head-dresses
so delicate, so hardy.
They were in no hurry. For ten months
the puckered corms lay like fat purses
in their bowl of earth, unopened gifts.
Now, when you have been long in the ground,
they rise, the flags you had planted,
flying once more your colours.

Anna Wigley lives in Cardiff, where she works for George Thomas Hospice Care. In addition to her three collections of poetry she has published a volume of short stories, *Footprints* (Gomer, 2004). She won the Geoffrey Dearmer Prize in 2000 and Second Prize in the Academi Cardiff International Poetry Competition in 2008.

Waking in Winter – Anna Wigley's third volume of poetry –
is a collection of celebrations and laments, lyrics to the living
and dead. Attuned to the pressures of history, these poems
explore grief, love and the uncanniness of the everyday.
Bringing together pieces on themes as diverse as missing cats,
car advertisements and Chinese foot-binding, the collection
displays a playfulness alongside more elegiac and nostalgic
moods. As in her previous collections, *The Bird Hospital* (2002)
and *Dürer's Hare* (2005), the author continues to eschew
fashionably vernacular accents and ironies in favour of a
personal, authentic voice and a spiritual engagement with her
environment, both urban and rural. At the same time, *Waking
in Winter* displays an expansion of range and a sharper edge that
establish Anna Wigley as a literary force to be reckoned with.

Praise for Anna Wigley:

'A bright and rising star of
English-language poetry in this decade'
Robin Young, *Planet*

'A quietly forceful poetic identity'
Tiffany Atkinson, *New Welsh Review*

£7.99

www.gomer.co.uk
Cover Image **Llinos Lanini**

ISBN 978-1-84323-970-3

9 781843 239703